Happy Chinese New Year!

Gung Hay Fat Choy!

This means "May prosperity be with you," and is a traditional Chinese New Year greeting.

Because the Chinese year is based on the movements of the Moon rather than the Sun, the Chinese New Year doesn't start on January 1—this year it falls on February 7!

The Chinese New Year traditionally marks the end of winter and the start of spring, and so it is a time for celebration and fun. It's also a time for family reunions, when ancestors are remembered and honored, and for asking the gods for their blessings.

A kumquat looks like a miniature orange, but it tastes a little bit sour.

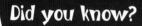

Did you know?

China is a powerful manufacturing country and makes 60 percent of the world's bicycles. Some economists believe that China will become the world's wealthiest nation by 2012—the year of the Dragon (see next page.)

Preparations
Because the New Year is a family celebration, special attention is paid to making the home beautiful. It is cleaned from top to bottom and special New Year food is cooked.

Orange-colored fruits
These bright fruits— oranges, tangerines, kumquats—are displayed in the home because of their color, which symbolizes good luck and joy.

Street parades

All over the world where the Chinese New Year is celebrated, street parades are held featuring processions, floats, and, of course, dancing dragons. The dragon is important because it symbolizes long life and prosperity.

Family name

Good luck message

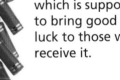

Lucky money

Chinese children and unmarried adults receive "lucky money" on New Year's morning. Inside the red and gold envelopes is pretend money, which is supposed to bring good luck to those who receive it.

Fireworks

Exploding fireworks are traditionally part of the New Year celebrations. Where real fireworks might be dangerous, plastic replicas, like these, are displayed in the home instead.

The Chinese Calendar

The ancient Chinese calendar has been used for thousands of years to analyse people's characters and to predict their futures.

Red is the main color for clothes at New Year because it is associated with joy and happiness

The calendar works on a 12-year cycle, with each year represented by a different animal. Each new year starts on the first day of the Chinese calendar, which is usually in February, and lasts for 15 days. The girl shown here was born in the year of the Rabbit. This means she is hardworking, pleasant, and obedient. When she grows up, the calendar predicts that she will be tranquil, generous, and imaginative.

The animals and what they mean

Year of the Rat
Equivalent to: 1912, 1924, 1936, 1948, 1960, 1972, 1984, 1996, 2008, 2020.
Characteristics: People born in the year of the Rat work hard to achieve their goals, but are also easily angered.
Compatibility: You should be compatible with those born in the years of the Dragon, Monkey, and Ox.

Year of the Ox
Equivalent to: 1913, 1925, 1937, 1949, 1961, 1973, 1985, 1997, 2009, 2021.
Characteristics: Ox people inspire confidence, though they can also be easily angered.
Compatibility: You should be compatible with those born in the years of the Snake, Rooster, and Rat.

Year of the Tiger
Equivalent to: 1914, 1926, 1938, 1950, 1962, 1974, 1986, 1998, 2010, 2022.
Characteristics: If you are a tiger person you are sensitive and sympathetic, but also short-tempered.
Compatibility: You should be compatible with those born in the years of the Horse, Dragon, and Dog.

Year of the Rabbit
Equivalent to: 1915, 1927, 1939, 1951, 1963, 1975, 1987, 1999, 2011, 2023.
Characteristics: Rabbit people are reserved and calm, but they are also fond of gossip.
Compatibility: You should be compatible with those born in the years of the Ram, Pig, and Dog.

Year of the Dragon
Equivalent to: 1916, 1928, 1940, 1952, 1964, 1976, 1988, 2000, 2012, 2024.
Characteristics: You are likely to be energetic, healthy, and excitable, but also stubborn.
Compatibility: You should be compatible with those born in the years of the Rat, Snake, and Monkey.

Year of the Snake
Equivalent to: 1917, 1929, 1941, 1953, 1965, 1977, 1989, 2001, 2013, 2025.
Characteristics: Snake people are wise and lucky with money, although they hate to fail at anything.
Compatibility: You should be compatible with those born in the years of the Ox, Dragon, and Rooster.

Year of the Horse
Equivalent to: 1918, 1930, 1942, 1954, 1966, 1978, 1990, 2002, 2014, 2026.
Characteristics: Horse people are good with their hands, but they can also be impatient and hot-blooded.
Compatibility: You should be compatible with those born in the years of the Tiger, Dog, and Ram.

Year of the Ram
Equivalent to: 1919, 1931, 1943, 1955, 1967, 1979, 1991, 2003, 2015, 2027.
Characteristics: You are likely to be a good artist, although shy and pessimistic.
Compatibility: You should be compatible with those born in the years of the Rabbit, Pig, and Horse.

Year of the Monkey
Equivalent to: 1920, 1932, 1944, 1956, 1968, 1980, 1992, 2004, 2016, 2028.
Characteristics: Monkey people are clever and skilful, but also impulsive and easily discouraged.
Compatibility: You should be compatible with those born in the years of the Dragon and Rat.

Year of the Rooster
Equivalent to: 1921, 1933, 1945, 1957, 1969, 1981, 1993, 2005, 2017, 2029.
Characteristics: Rooster people are often brave and are prepared to speak out for what they believe.
Compatibility: You should be compatible with those born in the years of the Ox, Snake, and Dragon.

Year of the Dog
Equivalent to: 1922, 1934, 1946, 1958, 1970, 1982, 1994, 2006, 2018, 2030.
Characteristics: People born in this year are loyal and trustworthy, though they can also be stubborn.
Compatibility: You should be compatible with those born in the years of the Horse, Tiger, and Rabbit.

Year of the Pig
Equivalent to: 1923, 1935, 1947, 1959, 1971, 1983, 1995, 2007, 2019, 2031.
Characteristics: As well as being honest, Pig people are inquisitive and always want to know "Why?"
Compatibility: You should be compatible with those born in the years of the Rabbit and Ram.

Make Your Party
Invitations

If you are celebrating the Chinese New Year with a party, the first thing you need are some invitations to send to your friends. Homemade invitations are much more fun than store-bought ones and you can make them to fit the theme of your party.

On each invitation, write the name of the person you are inviting to your party, then your name, the date and time of the party, and the address where it is being held. If you want a reply to the invitation, write RSVP at the bottom of it. This is French for *répondez s'il vous plaît*, which means "please respond" or "please reply."

You will need

- Scissors
- Ruler
- Pencil
- Thin card
- Glue stick
- Colored paper

Concertina invitation

1 Cut out a piece of colored paper 21 x 4 in. Make a fold 3 in from one end of it, and then fold the paper every 3 in to pleat it.

2 Draw a figure on the top fold of the paper. Make sure that its feet and legs don't go over the sides of the paper. With an adult helping, cut around the figure with the scissors.

3 Open the paper out. You will have a row of figures all joined together. Make a folded card. Glue the figure at the end inside the card on the left side.

Animal invitation

1 Draw large animals—such as the crocodile and dinosaur shown here—on colored paper. Then, with an adult helping, cut them out using the scissors.

2 Cut up different colored papers to make the details, such as the scales, claws, and eyes. Glue them into position on your animal cut-outs.

3 Fold each one in half widthways, then in half again. There should be three folds down each card.

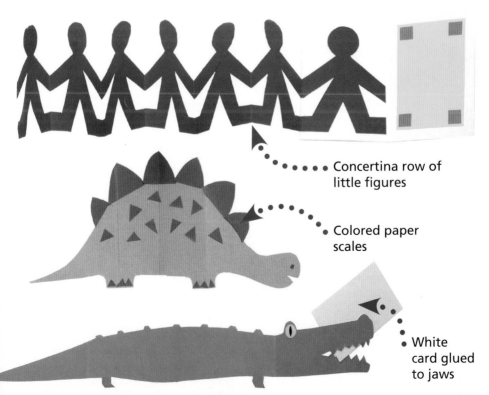

Concertina row of little figures

Colored paper scales

White card glued to jaws

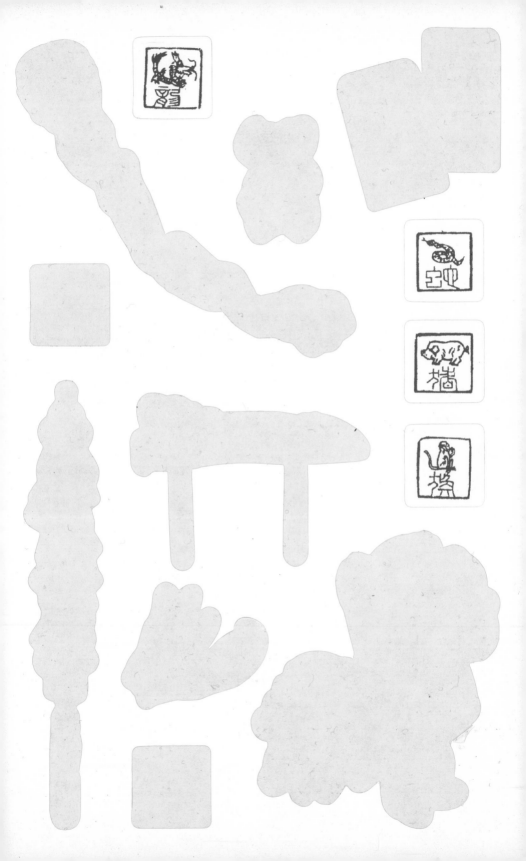

Games and Puzzles

True or false?

Do you know which of the following questions are true and which are false?

A
China has the second largest population of any country in the world.
True or false?

B
The Great Wall of China is the only man-made structure that can be seen from Outer Space.
True or false?

C
Ice cream was invented in China about 4,000 years ago.
True or false?

D
There are approximately 25,000 different written characters in the Chinese language.
True or false?

For answers to all puzzles, see page 16.

Amazing Fact

The world record for the longest Chinese dancing dragon was set in February 2000, at the Great Wall of China—it measured an incredible 1.89 miles in length!

Animal years

See if you can match the following years with the correct animals from the Chinese calendar. (Hint: look back at pages 4–5.)

1 1956 —

2 2007 —

3 1951 —

4 1936 —

5 1991 —

6 2029 —

7 2000 —

8 1913 —

9 2002 —

10 1994 —

11 2010 —

12 2013 —

Spot the difference

There are at least six changes in the bottom picture here. See how many you can find.

Chinese Cooking

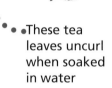

In China, food and cooking have been celebrated since early times. Feasts formed an important part of Chinese life and wealthy people often enjoyed elaborate banquets.

In contrast, for most of the year ordinary people lived on a simple diet of pulses (peas, beans, and lentils) and vegetables, with very little meat. Though rice was a favorite staple food in China, people living in the north ate mainly millet and some wheat. But both rich and poor Chinese preferred their food flavored with a wide variety of herbs and spices. To save fuel, food was chopped into small pieces and cooked quickly in an iron frying pan, or *wok*, for only a few minutes. Many foods were also steamed or stewed. Today, Chinese food is enjoyed throughout the world by Chinese and non-Chinese alike.

These tea leaves uncurl when soaked in water

Time for tea

Tea, or *cha*, has been grown in China for more than 2,000 years. The Chinese drank their tea from teabowls (not cups or mugs), which rested on lacquer bowl stands.

Chili peppers are traditionally added to hot, spicy dishes in southwestern China

Rice can be used to make wine as well as cakes and puddings

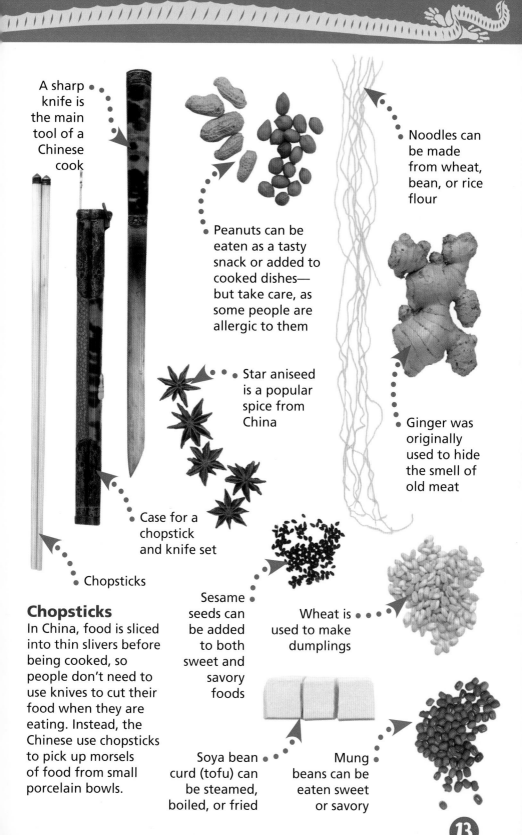

A sharp knife is the main tool of a Chinese cook

Peanuts can be eaten as a tasty snack or added to cooked dishes—but take care, as some people are allergic to them

Noodles can be made from wheat, bean, or rice flour

Ginger was originally used to hide the smell of old meat

Star aniseed is a popular spice from China

Case for a chopstick and knife set

Chopsticks

Sesame seeds can be added to both sweet and savory foods

Wheat is used to make dumplings

Chopsticks

In China, food is sliced into thin slivers before being cooked, so people don't need to use knives to cut their food when they are eating. Instead, the Chinese use chopsticks to pick up morsels of food from small porcelain bowls.

Soya bean curd (tofu) can be steamed, boiled, or fried

Mung beans can be eaten sweet or savory

The Cosmic Egg

This is a traditional Chinese tale about the creation of the world we know today. It uses some words you may not be familiar with, such as Yin and Yang. Ancient Chinese philosophy tells us that all things are a combination of opposites—Yin and Yang. Yin is negative, cold, dark, heavy, and feminine; Yang is positive, warm, bright, light, and masculine. The symbol for Yin and Yang is an egg divided into yolk and white, dark and light—Yin and Yang.

At the beginning of time, all was chaos, and this chaos was shaped like a hen's egg. Inside the egg were Yin and Yang, the two opposing forces of which the universe is made. One day, the warring energies inside the egg ripped it apart. The heavier elements sank, forming the earth, and

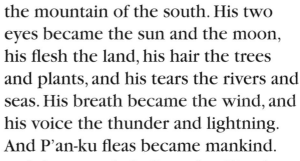

the lighter ones floated, forming the sky. And between the earth and sky was P'an-ku (Pan-Koo), the first being. Every day for 18,000 years, the earth and the sky separated a little farther, and every day P'an-ku grew at the same rate, so that he always filled the space between them.

P'an-ku's body was covered in hair and he had two horns thrusting from his forehead and two tusks from his upper jaw. When he was happy, the weather was fine, but if he became troubled or angry, it rained or there was a storm.

There are vaious stories about what happened to P'an-ku. Some say that, exhausted by the labor of keeping the earth and sky apart, he died. His body split, and his head became the mountain of the north, his stomach the mountain of the center, his left arm the mountain of the east, his right arm the mountain of the west, and his feet

the mountain of the south. His two eyes became the sun and the moon, his flesh the land, his hair the trees and plants, and his tears the rivers and seas. His breath became the wind, and his voice the thunder and lightning. And P'an-ku fleas became mankind.

Other people believe that P'an-ku lived and ruled mankind for a long time. Every day he instructed them from his throne until they knew about the sun and the moon and the stars above, and the four seas below. Listening to him, people lost their tiredness.

One morning, when the great P'an-ku had passed on all his wisdom to mankind, he disappeared and was never heard of again.

Fantasy creation

This fearsome kite has a dragon's head and a snake's body. Although it is very long, it is aerodynamically designed to help it fly well.

Kites

T**he Chinese probably invented kites some 3,000 years ago.**

In the Han dynasty (about 2,000 years ago) kites were used to frighten the enemy in battle, but later kites were flown to celebrate festivals. Kites were often made in animal shapes and could be very long indeed.

Combat
Fighting kites like these have blades in their tails to cut their opponent's lines.

Dragons
A popular decorative design for kites is the dragon.

Animal design
This kite makes a strange-looking flying fish.

Answers to puzzles on pages 10–11
Animal years: 1 Monkey; 2 Pig; 3 Rabbit; 4 Rat; 5 Ram; 6 Rooster; 7 Dragon; 8 Ox; 9 Horse; 10 Dog; 11 Tiger; 12 Snake.
True or false?: A False. The world's second-largest population is in India—China has the largest; B False—the Great Wall is too narrow to see from outer space and it is almost the same color as the background; C True; D False—there are more than 40,000 characters.